LIVES HERE?

MOUNTAINS

Mary-Jane Wilkins

BROWN BEAR BOOKS

Published by Brown Bear Books Ltd

4877 N. Circulo Bujia
Tucson, AZ 85718
USA

and

First Floor
9–17 St Albans Place
London N1 0NX

© 2017 Brown Bear Books Ltd

ISBN 978-1-78121-348-3

Library of Congress Cataloging-in-Publication Data available on request

Picture Researcher: Clare Newman
Designer: Melissa Roskell
Design Manager: Keith Davis
Editorial Director: Lindsey Lowe
Children's Publisher: Anne O'Daly

Printed in China

Picture Credits

The photographs in this book are used by permission and through the courtesy of:

Front Cover: tl, ©Shutterstock/ Dennis W. Donohue; cl, ©Shutterstock/ Targn Pleiades; br, ©Shutterstock/ Josh Schutz; c, ©Shutterstock/06photo; br, ©Shutterstock/ Hung Chung Chih.
Inside: 1, ©Shutterstock/Brykaylo Kuriy; 4, ©Shutterstock/Josh Schutz; 4-5, ©Shutterstock/ Daniel Predek; 6, ©Shutterstock/Tom Tietz; 6-7, ©Shutterstock/Sarah Jessup; 8, ©Shutterstock /Jeannette Katzir Photography; 8-9, ©Shutterstock/Dennis W. Donohue; 10, ©Shutterstock/JPL Designs; 10-11, © Shutterstock/Brendan van Son; 12, ©Shutterstock/Tardn Pleiades; 13, ©Shutterstock/E Alisa; 14, ©Shutterstock/ Maria Kraynova; 15, ©Shutterstock/Dmusjman; 16, ©Shutterstock/Volt Collection; 16-17, ©FLPA/Mitsuaki Iwaga/Minden Pictures; 18, ©Shutterstock/Tom Reichner; 18-19, ©Shutterstock/BG Smith; 20, ©Photoshot/All Canada Photos; 20-21, ©Shutterstock/Mark Medcalf; 22, ©Shutterstock/Alexey Kamenskiy; 23, ©Shutterstock/Photoshooter2015.
T=Top, C=Center, B=Bottom, L=Left, R=Right

Brown Bear Books has made every attempt to contact the copyright holder. If you have any information please contact:
licensing@brownbearbooks.co.uk

CONTENTS

Where Are the HIGHEST MOUNTAINS?

The highest mountains in the world are the Himalayas in southern Asia. Mountains are very cold and windy places. It is hard for animals to survive there.

Mountain goats have thick white coats that keep out the cold.

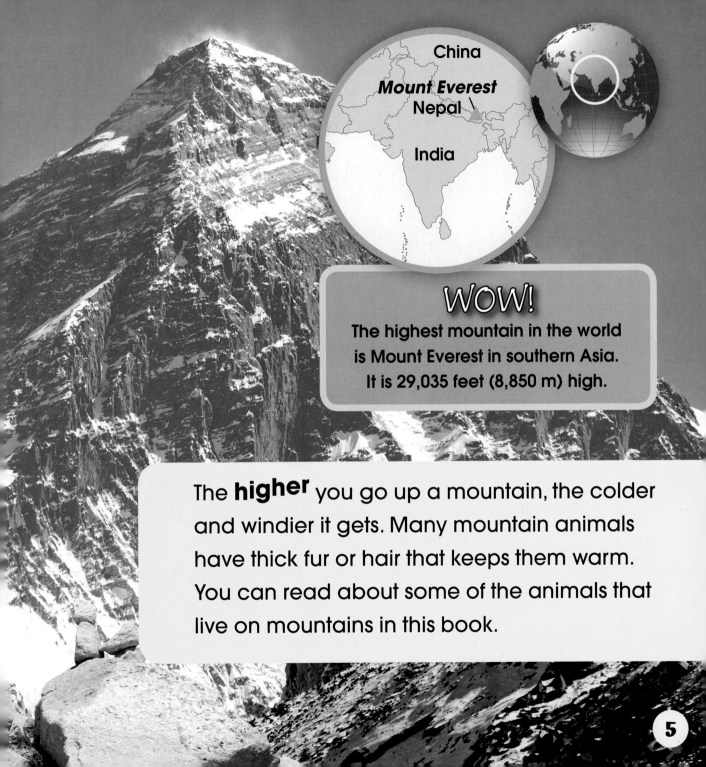

China

Mount Everest
Nepal

India

WOW!

The highest mountain in the world
is Mount Everest in southern Asia.
It is 29,035 feet (8,850 m) high.

The **higher** you go up a mountain, the colder
and windier it gets. Many mountain animals
have thick fur or hair that keeps them warm.
You can read about some of the animals that
live on mountains in this book.

BIGHORN SHEEP

These tough sheep live in the Rocky Mountains in North America. They have **big** curving horns that can weigh 30 pounds (14 kg).

Lambs are born in spring. They can walk soon after they are born.

WOW!
Bighorn sheep have hooves that help them grip icy, rocky surfaces.

Male sheep are called rams. They fight to see who is the strongest. They *charge* toward each other and **clash** horns.

SNOW LEOPARD

The snow leopard is the biggest cat in the Himalayas. It has thick gray hair, **w i d e** furry feet, and very strong legs. This big cat can leap up to 30 feet (9 m). It uses its long tail for balance.

A snow leopard's tail can be 36 inches (91 cm) long.

A snow leopard is a predator. Its coat has dark gray rings. The rings make the animal hard to see against the rocky mountain when it is hunting for prey.

ANDEAN CONDOR

This condor is one of the **biggest** flying birds in the world. Its huge wings can be 10.5 feet (3.2 m) from tip to tip.

Condors feed on carrion. That is the dead bodies of animals, such as sheep.

Condors are **heavy** birds.
They can weigh 33 pounds (15 kg).
These birds live in high places
where they can g l i d e
on the wind.

HIGHLAND COW

Highland cows have shaggy brown hair and **long** sweeping horns.

The first Highland cows were bred in Scotland, but now they live all over the world.

This tough cow can live for 18 years or more.

A male yak's horns can be 37 inches (95 cm) long.

YAK

Yaks have **long** brown-black hair. A large male can be 6.5 feet (2 m) tall at the shoulders.

Yaks graze on grass in the summer. In winter they dig under the snow with their horns to find moss and lichen to eat.

MOUNTAIN CAMEL

Most camels live in hot dry places, but Bactrian camels live on mountains in Asia. Here it can be as cold as –20°F (–29°C) in winter. Camels can go for a long time without drinking. This helps them survive when the water turns into ice.

The fat stored in the camel's humps help it make water.

Snow monkeys keep warm in the hot springs around a volcano.

SNOW MONKEY

The snow monkey lives in cold, high mountains in Japan. It has brown-gray fur and a short tail. Its hands and face are red. Snow monkeys eat twigs and bark.

GIANT PANDA

Giant pandas live high in the mountains in China. They hide away in thick, damp forests. Here they sit and munch bamboo all day.

WOW!
A panda can eat 30 pounds (14 kg) of bamboo a day!

Pandas are good at climbing trees, and they swim well, too.

PIKA

This furry animal is like a small rabbit. It lives in high mountains in North America and central Asia.

A pika is about 6 inches (15 cm) long. It could fit on an adult human's hand.

A pika has **long** gray-brown fur
and very furry feet. In the summer
pikas pick plants and carry them
to their dens. They store them
there to eat during the snowy winter.

PTARMIGAN

These birds live in the snowy mountains of North America. They eat tree leaves and flowers in the summer. In the winter they eat twigs and buds.

Chicks hatch in summer. Then the mother's feathers are gray and brown.

In the winter the ptarmigan's feathers turn white. This makes the birds hard to see against the snow. Predators can't see them easily.

MOUNTAIN FACTS

Mountains cover one-fifth of the Earth.

There is a higher mountain than Mount Everest that is mostly under the sea. This is Mauna Kea in Hawaii. It is 33,000 feet (10,000 m) high.

Sunshine is much stronger high up a mountain than beside the sea.

The wind is twice as strong at the top of a mountain as at the bottom.

Trees on mountains are shaped like cones. They have a strong trunk in the middle and the branches slope down to the ground.

USEFUL WORDS

carrion
The dead bodies of animals.
Condors feed on carrion. →

lichen
A living thing that grows on
rocks, dead wood, and the
ground. Yaks eat lichen in winter.

predator
An animal that hunts and kills other animals
for food. The snow leopard is a predator.

prey
An animal hunted and eaten by another
animal. The pika is prey for a snow leopard.

FIND OUT MORE

Discover Science: Mountains,
Margaret Hynes, Kingfisher 2012

Exploring Mountains
Anita Ganeri, Raintree, 2015

Life Cycles: Moutain Sean Callery,
Kingfisher, 2013

Who Can Live in the Mountains?
Sheila Anderson, Lerner, 2010

INDEX